W0259678

Gilmore girls

Life Lessons

THE OFFICIAL GUIDE TO LOVE, FRIENDSHIP, AND COFFEE

Written by Laurie Ulster

Contents

"You're not as clever as you think you are."

Emily Gilmore to Lorelai Gilmore

S7 E10 MERRY FISTICUFFS

Introduction

After combing through advice from the population of a certain quaint little town called Stars Hollow, it seems Lorelai Gilmore may indeed be as clever as she thinks. Whether you're learning from their successes or their setbacks, you'll find wisdom in the words—and sometimes contradictory actions—of Lorelai and Rory, Luke and Jess, Michel and Sookie, Lane and Mrs. Kim, Miss Patty, Babette, Paris, Dean... and of course, Kirk. They have all sorts of opinions on life, love, career, school, families, food, and more—everything you need to get you through life's daily struggles. Pair it with a cup of coffee, and you're good to go.

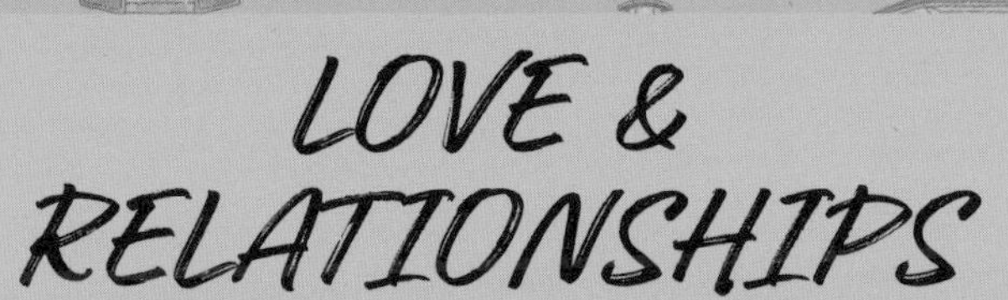

"I just want you to know I'm in. I'm all in."

Luke Danes
S5 E3 WRITTEN IN THE STARS

"I have liked you for some time now and I don't think this feeling is going to go away."

Lane Kim

S5 E4 TIPPECANOE AND TAYLOR, TOO

LOVE & RELATIONSHIPS

Making the first move

You can't always tell if someone likes you back or not. If you want to know where you stand romantically, you might have to make the first move. After attempting to suppress her feelings for Zack, Lane tells him outright that she thinks of him as "more than a bandmate and more than a friend." Once Zack has time to digest it, he's all in. So if you need to know, take that step! Bid on a lunch basket like Jess, ask someone to dance at a wedding, interrupt a squash blossom rant to ask for a date. That said, make sure you do it in a considerate and respectful way. We're talking to you, Tristan Dugray and Jason Stiles.

WHAT WOULD KIRK DO?

KIRK WOULD HAVE HIS FIRST DATE AT HIS MOM'S HOUSE.

DON'T DO THAT.

"You should've told me, Richard."

Emily Gilmore

S6 E6 WELCOME TO THE DOLLHOUSE

LOVE & RELATIONSHIPS

Don't keep secrets

When you're in a relationship with someone, it's best to be on the same side. Things can get tough when you keep secrets from each other, and the residents of Stars Hollow and their families are no strangers to a secret. Luke doesn't tell Lorelai that he has a daughter, Richard doesn't tell Emily that he has lunch with his ex-girlfriend Pennilyn Lott every year, and Logan doesn't tell Rory when his company falls apart. It can be hurtful to find out that your partner is hiding things from you, even if you think it will protect them. So open up. If you're carrying around a big secret, you might want to go get your partner and spill it. You'll probably feel better in the long run too!

"I'm not saying wallowing will help you get over Dean. It's part of the process."

Lorelai Gilmore

S1 E17 THE BREAKUP: PART 2

LOVE & RELATIONSHIPS

The box

For some, the process for breakups involves multiple tissues and wallowing, but here's an alternative step: the box. When Rory and Dean first break up, Lorelai stores everything Rory wanted to throw away that reminded her of Dean in a box hidden at the back of their closet. You might want to purge everything that reminds you of your ex, but the box is better. When it goes on the shelf (preferably hidden by some coats) and the door shuts, you can shut your own door. Wallow for a bit, then step back into the world. Whenever you're ready for those memories, the box awaits!

"There are just a lot of things right now in my life that are undecided. And that used to scare me, but now I kind of like the idea that it's just all kind of wide open."

Rory Gilmore

S7 E21 UNTO THE BREACH

LOVE & RELATIONSHIPS

Enjoy the single life

No matter what society expects, you don't have to be attached. Being single is underrated. Embrace it! You can go wherever opportunity leads, and no one gets jealous if you want to *Lady and the Tramp* your spaghetti with someone new. Make plans around what's best for you and not what fits in with someone else's plan. You don't have to settle down and get married just to get an avocado tree in your backyard—grow your own tree and make guacamole whenever the mood strikes. Go on a spontaneous road trip, head to a Bangles concert with your friends, or curl up Rory-style with a great book. The world is your oyster, and one doesn't have to be the loneliest number after all.

"You have your ex-boyfriend's number in your cell phone?"

Louise Grant

S4 E17 GIRLS IN BIKINIS, BOYS DOIN' THE TWIST

LOVE & RELATIONSHIPS

Can you be friends with your exes?

When Rory and Dean try to be friends after he marries Lindsay, it ends in catastrophe because they're still in love with each other. It can be really hard trying to be friends when you're not sure if the flame has gone out. But once the romance is in the past, an ex can be the one person who will tell you the truth when you most need to hear it. It's Jess who snaps Rory out of her Daughters-of-the-American-Revolution-era, something Lorelai and Logan couldn't do. If you and your ex still care about each other and can get past any residual awkwardness, you could find a deep, true friendship worth holding onto.

"Seriously, you've got one minute to make an impression and that's all you can come up with?"

Paris Geller

S5 E10 BUT NOT AS CUTE AS PUSHKIN

Dropping your defenses

Paris has been perfecting the art of self-defense since she was a kid. She's built up so much protective shielding that she doesn't realize when she's asked out on her very first date. When Paris is willing to try speed dating at Yale, it leads her to Doyle, who's just as keen on self-protection as she is—hence their mutual interest in martial arts, and each other. It can be a mistake to sacrifice the chance for real connections with people because you're afraid they won't like you. If you want to, put yourself out there. It might just pay off.

FAMILY & FRIENDSHIP
"Nothing wrong with a strange but loving household."
Lorelai Gilmore
S7 E10 MERRY FISTICUFFS

"This is all the stuff I ran away from. I just assumed you'd be running with me."

Lorelai Gilmore to Rory Gilmore
S2 E8 THE INS AND OUTS OF INNS

FAMILY & FRIENDSHIP

Carving their own path

When Emily gives Lorelai the lavish upbringing that she relished herself, Lorelai runs away, despising the pressures and pageantry. Lorelai attempts to keep Rory far from the world she fled, then boom! One day Rory's walking down an elegant staircase into Hartford society, fan dance and all. You might find that those you care for end up desiring a life that's very different from the one you had hoped for them. Everyone has to carve their own path. What's important is that you are there to offer your love and support.

"The room...
It smells like guilt
and Chanel No. 5."

Lorelai Gilmore

S4 E3 THE HOBBIT, THE SOFA, AND DIGGER STILES

FAMILY & FRIENDSHIP

Don't overdo it

When Emily throws Rory a 16th birthday party, she thinks she knows best and invites the whole of Rory's Chilton class—most of whom Rory doesn't even know very well, or like! Years later, Emily completely redecorates Rory's Yale dorm without asking her (something Lorelai smelled a mile away), bulldozing over who Rory really is and making her feel uncomfortable. Emily's actions come from a place of love, but she should have asked first. If you try to take too much control over someone's life, you might stand in the way of letting them figure out what they do or don't want for themselves.

"There's no great time to be a parent, Luke; you just are one."

Anna Nardini

S6 E12 JUST LIKE GWEN AND GAVIN

FAMILY & FRIENDSHIP

Second chances

Life is full of surprises. Sometimes one of those surprises is becoming a dad when you're 16, like Christopher, or meeting your daughter for the first time when she asks for one of your hairs for her middle school science project, like Luke. After missing out on large parts of Rory's childhood, Christopher's determined to be involved in Gigi's life from the beginning. Luke also learns to become a dad to April, handling the highs, the lows, and everything in between. Learning you're a parent further down the line doesn't mean it's too late. You can still develop a relationship with your child if that's what you both want, as long as you respect their boundaries.

WHAT WOULD KIRK DO?

KIRK WOULD GET A CAT, NAME IT AFTER HIMSELF, THEN LIVE IN MORTAL FEAR OF IT.

DON'T DO THAT.

"So you'd rather have your house fall down than let your mother help you?"

Emily Gilmore

S2 E11 SECRETS AND LOANS

FAMILY & FRIENDSHIP

Asking for help when you need it

It can feel like the hardest thing you've ever had to do—even harder than convincing Luke to redecorate the diner—but every once in a while, even after you grow up, you might need to ask for help from your parents. Whether you need someone to look after you when you have a back spasm, help with tuition money, or even give you the phone number of a handsome guy you met at an event, the last people you want to admit you need help from might be the best people for the job. Let them in, ask for what you need, and be prepared to give up your Friday nights.

"Now you get your do-over. A new and improved Lorelai. Congrats."

Lorelai Gilmore

S6 E1 NEW AND IMPROVED LORELAI

FAMILY & FRIENDSHIP

Breaking cycles

It's good to learn from the mistakes of the past, but it doesn't always happen. When Rory drops out of Yale, she flees Stars Hollow as Lorelai once fled Hartford and heads right for Emily and Richard's doorstep. They think she belongs with them, but while Emily gloats about breaking up Thelma and Louise, history repeats anew. Emily drives Rory away exactly the way she did with Lorelai because she makes all the same mistakes. It's hard to break a cycle unless you take some responsibility for how you got to where you are. If you don't change anything along the way, you're unlikely to get a new outcome.

“We are best friends first and mother and daughter second.”

Lorelai Gilmore
S2 E16 THERE’S THE RUB

FAMILY & FRIENDSHIP

Should you be your kid's best friend?

Should your kid be the Joel to your Ethan? The Damon to your Affleck? The jury's still out on this one, although it's obvious why Lorelai raised Rory the way she did. The last thing Lorelai wanted was for Rory to have the same disconnect she had with her parents. As long as you foster room for them to make their own friends, it can be great to have that kind of relationship. If you provide loving and dependable care for your child, hopefully they will appreciate not just your friendship but your guidance, too.

WHAT WOULD MISS PATTY DO?

SHE'D PUT HER KID IN DANCE CLASSES TO KEEP THEM AT HER SIDE AND WORRY ABOUT THE REST LATER.

STARS HOLLOW
FOUNDED · 1779 ·

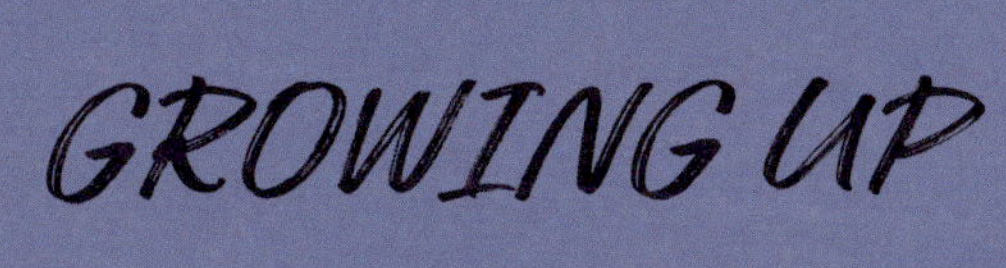

"You have so many years of screwups ahead of you."

Lorelai Gilmore

S1 E8 LOVE AND WAR AND SNOW

"But you... You provide for yourself. You're not dependent on anyone."

Emily Gilmore
S7 E15 I'M A KAYAK, HEAR ME ROAR

GROWING UP

Self-reliance

Even if you are lucky enough to have a safety net of loving, helpful friends or family, self-reliance can be a very useful tool. When Lorelai decides to put her needs first and leave home, she doesn't have anyone to rely on but herself. She finds a job as a hotel cleaner, then works her way up to running the Independence Inn. Along the way, she learns to sew like a pro, so when Rory needs a dress for her first dance, she gets one custom-made by her mom. We all may need help sometimes, but it can be a great feeling to learn self-reliance.

"I see you haven't changed, Lorelai."

Straub Hayden

S1 E15 CHRISTOPHER RETURNS

GROWING UP

Acting like a grown-up

It can be hard for your guardians to see you as an adult. They'll always remember the time when they had to do everything for you. So if you're still talking about Wile E. Coyote at the dinner table, they might keep treating you like a kid watching cartoons. If you want them to take you seriously, things may need to change. Acting like a grown-up might mean holding back on the nonstop punchlines (Lorelai), actually telling your parents who you're engaged to (Lorelai), or standing up for your wife when your mother picks on her (which Richard never does).

WHAT WOULD KIRK DO?

YOU MIGHT NOT HAVE TO SLEEP NAKED ON A BOAT IN A GARAGE ON YOUR PATH TO FULLY RECOGNIZED ADULTHOOD, BUT THAT IS WHAT WORKED FOR KIRK.

"This party's a testament to you, Lorelai, and the home you've created here."

Richard Gilmore

S7 E22 BON VOYAGE

GROWING UP

Leaving home

For some, the best way to move on from childhood is to leave home behind you. When Jess leaves Stars Hollow, he transitions from town bad boy into a successful writer and publisher. Lane has to move out so Mrs. Kim can see her as an aspiring musician, and Lorelai leaves Hartford behind and finds a community to help raise her daughter. Emily and Richard still judge almost everything Lorelai does—from her clothes to her life choices—but they're proud of her and what she's built for herself and Rory. Leaving home can be one of the hardest things you'll ever have to do, but you can always come back if that choice is right for you.

“I didn’t tell you because I knew you’d act like this.”

Lane Kim to Rory Gilmore

S2 E11 SECRETS AND LOANS

GROWING UP

Accepting people for who they are

One lesson you learn as you grow up is to accept your friends for who they are. As people grow, they might challenge the way you've always thought about them. Rory's been Lane's best friend since preschool, but Lane keeps her cheerleading a secret because Rory is judgmental about it. Rory also refuses to accept that Dean's life has changed, giving him a hard time for leaving school. Don't forget to look inward— most of us change. If staying their friend is what you want, true friendship might mean loving them for who they are, even if it's not what you expected.

"People can live a hundred years without really living for a minute."

Logan Huntzberger
S5 E7 YOU JUMP, I JUMP, JACK

GROWING UP

Taking risks

Growing up gives you perspective, and perspective teaches you that you might miss out if you play it safe *all* the time. Rory is used to looking in from the outside, but when she chases down Yale's secret society, she faces a moment of truth where she has to decide between watching things happen and leaping into the moment. When Rory jumps off a giant scaffold, umbrella in hand, it changes her. She experiences true exhilaration for the first time. You don't have to take it literally and jump off a scaffold, though. Some leaps are figurative!

"Wait, wait! Look around for a second."

Lorelai Gilmore
S3 E22 THOSE ARE STRINGS, PINOCCHIO

GROWING UP

Acknowledge your achievements

As you rush through life, don't forget to congratulate the person who's worked the hardest to get you where you are: you. Rory starts school at Chilton feeling as though she doesn't fit in and wonders if she'll ever make it into the college of her dreams. When Rory graduates, she stands in front of the class as their valedictorian. She and Lorelai find a moment to take it all in: the achievement and the fact that something that was once so intimidating isn't scary anymore. Try not to be so hard on yourself; along the way, you might find that you didn't win your golden ticket—you earned it!

MONEY
"If I had a dollar
for every time you
gave up..."
Emily Gilmore
S1 E6 RORY'S BIRTHDAY PARTIES

"If I want a plane, I'll buy a plane!"

Emily Gilmore

S6 E9 THE PRODIGAL DAUGHTER RETURNS

MONEY

Money can't buy love

Does Emily really need to buy Richard the most expensive mustache comb available at the mall? Spending cash might feel like the solution to all your problems, but that often isn't true. Logan doesn't win back Rory with coffee carts, flowers, or gifts. He has to humble himself at Lorelai's doorstep and beg for help to get Rory to even consider forgiveness. And Emily doesn't solve any of her problems by buying diamond watches. Money isn't an apology or a declaration of love, and it won't fill an emotional hole, no matter how many Venetian glass apples you can afford.

“Look at all these haughty people with their bags, just rubbing our faces in it.”

Lorelai Gilmore
S4 E15 SCENE IN A MALL

MONEY

Having fun on a budget

When you're low on funds, you can find lots of fun things to do, but window shopping, as Rory and Lorelai find out, is probably not one of them. It may sound glamorous to walk around the mall and check out the windows like Rosalind Russell and Ava Gardner walking down Fifth Avenue, especially if you go arm in arm. In the end, it's likely to turn out to be a lot more boring than it sounds. Take a stroll in the park, play games at home, get creative! There's still lots of fun to be had without spending a dime.

"Everything in a relationship isn't about money, Mom."

Lorelai Gilmore

S1 E18 THE THIRD LORELAI

MONEY

It's not always about money

Emily might think a $12 bracelet doesn't make a good present, but she couldn't be more wrong. Your gifts don't need to cost a fortune to prove you care about someone. A smorgasbord lunch at the food court can feel as special as a five-star meal if it's done with panache. And success isn't always defined by money, either. When Lane, Brian, and Zack are saving money by living together in their one-bedroom apartment, space is tight, but they are bonding in the true spirit of rock and roll. They're happy, and that can be a whole lot more valuable.

"But I'm loaded—
didn't you tell her?
I'm loaded!"

Christopher Hayden
S6 E10 HE'S SLIPPIN' 'EM BREAD ... DIG?

MONEY

Money can't fix everything

Finding dinner in Paris at 5 a.m. is a challenge that Christopher solves when he gets a restaurant to open just for him and Lorelai, complete with an Eiffel Tower view. If you're lucky enough to be able to afford such an extravagant gesture, splurging and taking someone away can be a really kind thing to do. However, often relationships need more than a trip to Paris to make them work. Christopher has a tendency to try to use his position of wealth as a quick fix for his problems, when the best thing for him to do might be to take a moment to listen to what the other person actually needs.

WHAT WOULD KIRK DO?

KIRK WOULD SAVE EVERY DOLLAR FROM EVERY JOB HE'S EVER HAD—AND HE WOULDN'T BRAG.

Happy Birthday
CHILTON

SCHOOL & WORK

"I study and then I think about studying and then I study some more."

Paris Geller

S1 E18 THE THIRD LORELAI

"I've been a resident of Faulkner's Yoknapatawpha County, hunted the white whale aboard the Pequod, fought alongside Napoleon, sailed a raft with Huck and Jim, committed absurdities with Ignatius J. Reilly, rode a sad train with Anna Karenina, and strolled down Swann's Way."

Rory Gilmore

S3 E22 THOSE ARE STRINGS, PINOCCHIO

SCHOOL & WORK

The joys of reading

In a world where any movie or TV show you want to watch is at your fingertips, it's easy to forget just how far a great book can take you. As well as following the action, reading a book can put you inside someone's head—as Rory points out in her valedictorian speech, you're ON that ship with Captain Ahab. It's Rory's love of books that piques Jess's interest, but that's just a bonus. Reading is a great way to activate your brain, learn empathy, and go on adventures no matter where you might find—or lose—yourself. Plus, it's something to do when you're stuck at a party you'd rather not be at.

"I like that woman!"

Emily Gilmore about Mrs. Kim

S1 E19 EMILY IN WONDERLAND

SCHOOL & WORK

Be a boss, not a tyrant

Whether you're a newbie antique buyer or a member of a rock band, if Mrs. Kim gives orders, you follow them. When Emily Gilmore tells you to give the bride your best wishes instead of your congratulations, you obey. At Emily and Mrs. Kim's first meeting, sparks of mutual respect fly. But there's danger, Will Robinson: wield your power wisely. Paris inspires a full-blown mutiny at the Yale Daily News when she issues everyone numbers (on hats!) and rewrites every line of copy until her staff rise up and oust her. Be fair, or you'll go through employees like Emily goes through terrified housekeepers.

WHAT WOULD KIRK DO?

KIRK WOULD SHOUT ALL HIS INSTRUCTIONS THROUGH A BULLHORN.

DON'T DO THAT.

"I did what I had to do… what Richard Gilmore would do."

Floyd Stiles

S4 E18 TICK, TICK, TICK, BOOM!

SCHOOL & WORK

Swimming with the sharks

Interested in the cutthroat world of business? Becoming a shark could mean swimming with those with sharper teeth. When Jason Stiles tries to get revenge on his father, Floyd, by teaming up with Richard Gilmore, it backfires. Floyd sweet-talks them into a dinner, then tells them he's suing them for everything thcy'vc got. Richard then betrays Jason, dismissing Lorelai's outrage with a Don Corleone–style "It's business." The lesson here is: don't conduct yourself like Richard, Floyd, or Jason. Treat people how you'd like to be treated, and avoid doing business with people who don't.

"Mom, Kirk's following us in a little clowny car."

Rory Gilmore

S4 E4 CHICKEN OR BEEF?

SCHOOL & WORK

Diversify

Kirk's been a filmmaker, termite exterminator, hockey announcer, mail carrier, security expert, dog walker, real estate agent, actor, engagement ring salesman, wedding DJ, notary, tow truck driver, town sash maker, and aspiring dance captain. He even agreed to jump out of a plane for Taylor's Olde Fashioned Soda Shoppe. Kirk is the poster boy for professional diversification if ever there was one. Some people figure out what they want to do with their professional lives early. But if you're not sure what your thing is going to be, that's okay! It can be useful to have more than one interest, and you can follow where they take you.

"So she offered us the job and I just took it!"

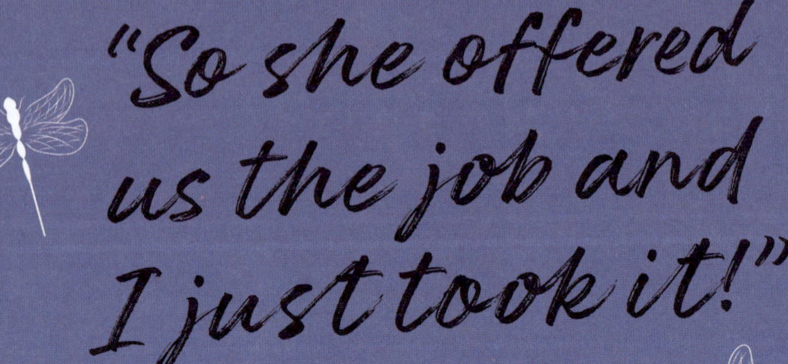

Sookie St. James
S4 E3 THE HOBBIT, THE SOFA, AND DIGGER STILES

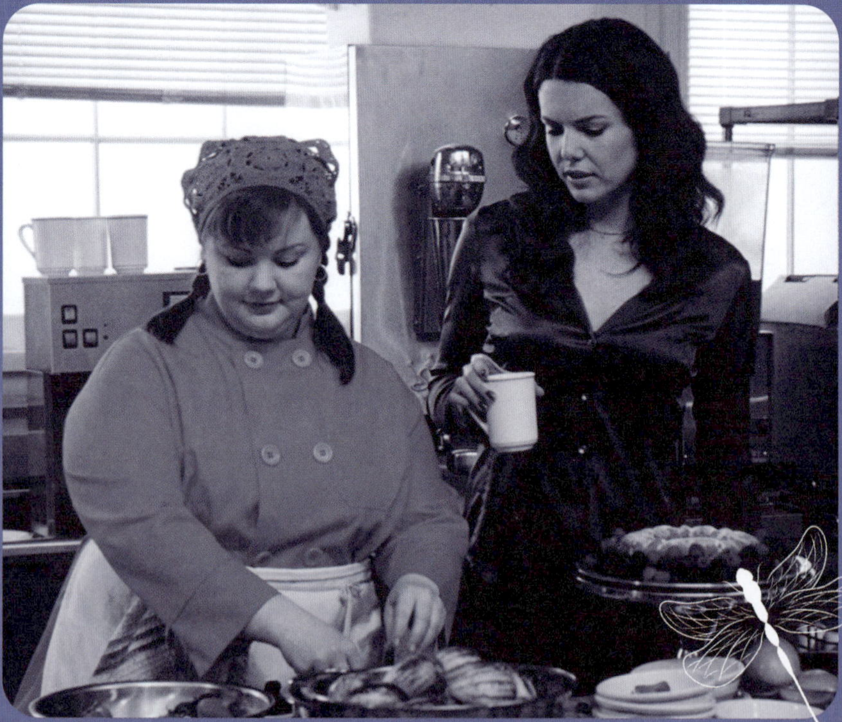

SCHOOL & WORK

The art of the pivot

When the Independence Inn closes, Sookie and Lorelai start up a catering business to help them get by. Facing some miserable Connecticut weather, Rory and Paris stop shunning spring break. They decide to get the college adventure by catching a ride to sunny Florida to experience everything it can throw at them. If the path you're on changes abruptly, pivot! You might find the skills and exposure to new things you gain could set you up for all kinds of success.

"I've always known exactly what is in front of me, and I've always known exactly where I'm going, and now... I don't know what's out there."

Rory Gilmore

S7 E7 FRENCH TWIST

SCHOOL & WORK

It's okay not to know what's next

As her Yale graduation date approaches, Rory starts to panic because she doesn't have anything lined up. Rory's spent her whole life working toward her goals and planning next steps, so she feels scared when she realizes she has no idea what lies ahead. Should she go to graduate school? Journalism school? Law school? Why does everyone else seem to know what they want when Rory is so uncertain? It's important to remember that it's okay if you don't know. You might finish your education and find yourself fretting about what to do with the next chapter in your life, but think of it as a wide-open horizon where anything is possible—maybe something you haven't even thought of yet.

"Coffee, please, and a shot of cynicism."

Lorelai Gilmore

S1 E16 STAR-CROSSED LOVERS AND OTHER STRANGERS

"How about coffee? You like coffee?"

"Only with my oxygen."

Max Medina and Lorelai Gilmore

S1 E5 CINNAMON'S WAKE

FOOD (& COFFEE)

The joys of coffee

Every love interest who wants to be in the life of a Gilmore girl must accept that coffee is part of the package. Lorelai and Max test the dating waters with a coffee, and Luke may serve Lorelai's cup of Joe with an eye roll, but he still reaches for the pot the moment he sees her at the diner door. Logan knows it's the path to Rory's heart; he charters an apology coffee cart to follow her around after an argument. It's delicious, life-affirming fuel. Maybe you don't need it in an IV, but if enjoyed in measure, coffee can be your friend.

"So you're fine with having no dinner tonight, is that it?"

"I certainly am not."

Emily Gilmore and Richard Gilmore
S1 E8 LOVE AND WAR AND SNOW

FOOD (& COFFEE)

How to navigate a food disaster

When a snowstorm changes their plans, Rory introduces Emily and Richard to the joys of parmesan-topped frozen pizza. Jason Stiles and Lorelai stock up on onion chips and pink marshmallow coconut balls when their fancy restaurant date doesn't work out and create a makeshift dinner to eat sitting outside the supermarket. You don't have to be Alain Ducasse! Don't let the fact that Plan A has gone awry ruin your night. Try something new or bring back a childhood favorite—there's much to discover in the last-minute scavenge.

"I never go anywhere without a casserole."

Sookie St. James

S6 E9 THE PRODIGAL DAUGHTER RETURNS

Expressing love through food

If words aren't your thing, take your cue from Sookie St. James and try serving your love on a plate. Sookie makes muffin tops (without the bottoms) and milkshakes for midnight guests. She shows up at Lorelai's with mini hot dogs, taquitos, and mac and cheese. And she marries Jackson, who is willing to sleep in the zucchini patch to ensure the Dragonfly Inn's opening night (and Sookie's critically acclaimed zucchini soup) will be nothing short of perfection.

"Bring your appetites, bring your opinions, and, uh, hey, someone bring some music."

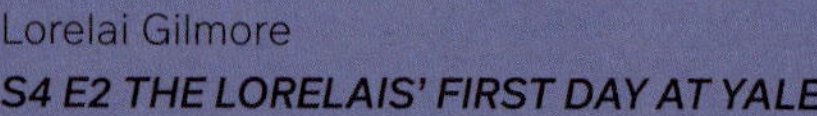

Lorelai Gilmore

S4 E2 THE LORELAIS' FIRST DAY AT YALE

FOOD (& COFFEE)

The art of takeout testing

When you're settling into a new place, one of the keys to understanding the lay of the land is mapping out your takeout options. If you've got a large number of ravenous guests, one way is to do it Lorelai-style. Her system is simple. The goal: Get a wide selection of the local takeout. The method: Order everything within delivery distance and make a chart so you can map out your 1–10 ratings for food quality and speed of delivery. Take note of menu highlights and don't forget to put it all in a chart for easy reference.

WHAT WOULD KIRK DO?

KIRK WOULD START HIS OWN RESTAURANT AND CALL IT "KIRK'S," OF COURSE.

"If eating cake is wrong, I don't want to be right."

Lorelai Gilmore
S2 E3 RED LIGHT ON THE WEDDING NIGHT

FOOD (& COFFEE)

Love the food you love

Food is extremely important to Lorelai and Rory. These two survive on a steady stream of cheeseburgers, pancakes, and tacos, and even when the pizza is on the way, they fill in the gap with appetizers: stacks of toaster pastries (around an apple). Once you've made the decision to eat the pie, enjoy it!
Billy Joel had two desserts when he visited the Independence Inn (according to Sookie), and that was after appetizers and a main course. Life is meant to be relished, although it might be a good idea to look outside of the pizza food groups.

"You can't watch Willy Wonka without massive amounts of junk food."

Lorelai Gilmore

S1 E7 KISS AND TELL

FOOD (& COFFEE)

Matching snacks to movies

Whether your movie features Vito Morgenstern or Viggo Mortensen, there's a special food to accompany it, and Lorelai knows what it is. For *Willy Wonka & the Chocolate Factory*, it's only natural for Rory and Lorelai to stock up on jelly beans, chocolate kisses, cookie dough, and that candy with the stick and the sugar to dip it in. Don't forget the marshmallows! Take a page out of the Gilmore book and try a slice of pizza with *Mystic Pizza*, or even a ratatouille with *Ratatouille*. The list goes on!

"Reality has absolutely no place in our world!"

Lorelai Gilmore
S4 E1 BALLROOMS AND BISCOTTI

"I'm going to the music store to look at things I can't afford."

Lane Kim

S4 E4 CHICKEN OR BEEF?

DREAMS & ASPIRATIONS

Hard work can pay off

Lane's big dream is to be a rock and roll star—no easy task when you grow up in a household where your favorite music is forbidden. Against all odds and with nothing to go on but her own instincts, Lane goes from gazing at a music store window to joining a band. She becomes a better drummer with every practice, gets a gig, and eventually moves in with her bandmates. Her music dreams are all going to come true one day, even if she isn't quite famous enough (yet!) to introduce Lorelai to Bono. If you want to achieve your dreams, you often have to do a lot more than wishing. Working hard and achieving your goals can often go hand in hand!

“And no matter how many crappy, stupid, useless assignments you throw at me, I'm not going to quit and I'm not going to back down.”

Rory Gilmore

S2 E5 NICK & NORA/SID & NANCY

DREAMS & ASPIRATIONS

Perseverance

Rory knows about persistence, whether it's taking a mundane subject and turning it into a bittersweet, touching article for *The Franklin* or trailing an editor around the *Stamford Eagle Gazette* until he gives her a job. She feels derailed after Mitchum Huntzberger tells her she doesn't have what it takes to be a journalist, but eventually Rory remembers who she is at her core: a person who doesn't give up. There will often be obstacles in your way. Taking the high road and doing your best with what you have will likely earn you respect from others and, more importantly, from yourself.

"But Harvard's all you've talked about for years."

Luke Danes
S3 E17 A TALE OF POES AND FIRE

DREAMS & ASPIRATIONS

It's okay to change your mind

Rory spends her whole life planning for Harvard. She works hard to get into Chilton and works even harder once she's there to get high grades and write for the school paper. When Rory gets into Harvard, Yale, and Princeton—facing a choice for the first time instead of just praying for acceptance—the Pro/Con list doesn't lie. Yale is the place for her, no matter how many Harvard pennants festoon her bedroom walls. Yes, hold on to your dreams, but if those dreams shift, that's okay! It doesn't mean that you've given up; it just means you're still learning and growing.

"You crushed that girl!"

"If she's got what it takes, she'll bounce back."

Richard Gilmore and Mitchum Huntzberger

S6 E5 WE'VE GOT MAGIC TO DO

Rebounding after a setback

When you've been blindsided like Rory is when Mitchum Huntzberger tells her she doesn't have what it takes to be a journalist, you might be tempted to take action that is more drastic than it should be. Rory believes every cruel word that comes out of Mitchum's mouth, convinces Logan to steal a yacht with her, and gets them both arrested. It can be hard not to take it personally when something hurtful is said to you, but try not to let a setback (or one person's opinion) send you into a full tailspin. Spend time with people who make you happy, tell someone how you're feeling, and definitely don't steal a yacht!

“I'm not going to Harvard. I got the tiny envelope.”

Paris Geller

S3 E16 THE BIG ONE

Try not to self-sabotage

The all-time self-sabotage championship title goes to Paris Geller, who has a habit of stepping into the spotlight just in time to go down in flames as publicly as possible. At the Chilton dance, she announces at top volume that she had to pay for her cousin's gas just to get him to accompany her there. A few years later, she's on television telling the world that she didn't get into Harvard. When you've had a disappointment, don't get in your own way! When you feel a self-destructive urge coming on, take a deep breath, reevaluate, and don't give in to it.

WHAT WOULD KIRK DO?

WHEN KIRK SEES THE BAD STUFF COMING, HE ENLISTS A PAL—USUALLY LUKE—TO HELP HIM OUT. GOOD ADVICE!

"Excuse me.
There's a phone call for you.
If I'm to fetch you like a dog,
I'd like a cookie and a raise."

Michel Gerard

S2 E1 SADIE, SADIE

DREAMS & ASPIRATIONS

Speak up for yourself

If you want something, sometimes it's wise to speak up for yourself. When Lorelai and Sookie finally get the Dragonfly Inn, they forget to update Michel, whom they'd always planned to bring with them. Even though he tries to downplay it later, it's Michel's call to Sookie that gets Lorelai and Sookie to find him in New York City to make it indisputably clear they want him back. There's a good way to make sure people know you want to work with them on that dream project, to stop taking advantage of you, or anything else—let them know. If you want something, go ahead and say it, or it might never happen!

EVERYDAY LIFE

"It's times like these that you realize what is truly important in your life."

Miss Patty

S3 E20 SAY GOODNIGHT, GRACIE

"I'm not getting married. No, it ain't for me. It's not in the cards."

Lorelai Gilmore at Lane Kim's wedding

S6 E19 I GET A SIDEKICK OUT OF YOU

EVERYDAY LIFE

It's not your day every day

There's something about weddings that seems to inspire embarassing moments. The combination of big feelings and large crowds has a tendency to bring secrets to the surface. At Lane's wedding, Lorelai takes the mic to toast the happy couple, but her speech quickly turns into a lament about how Lane is getting married before she is. Even though you might feel like you're the main character, when it comes to weddings, keep the spotlight on the couple in question!

"I gotta tell you, of all the nutty barn-raising shindigs this town can cook up, this one wasn't half bad."

Jess Mariano

S2 E13 A-TISKET, A-TASKET

EVERYDAY LIFE

Participate locally

Even if your town doesn't have its own Festival of Living Pictures where the locals pretend to be inside famous paintings, there are still ways to pitch in for town events. Every town needs a Miss Patty to train the kids dressed as dancing apples for the Cider Mill Parade, a Lorelai to sew costumes, or a Luke to build sets for *Fiddler on the Roof*. Rory humiliates herself at least six times a year in various costumes—all to be part of her community. Whether it's an annual dance marathon, a winter carnival, a lunch basket auction, or a snowman-building contest, there's always a way to contribute.

WHAT WOULD KIRK DO?

KIRK WOULD VOLUNTEER TO HIDE ALL THE EASTER EGGS FOR THE YEARLY HUNT BUT FORGET TO DRAW A MAP.

DON'T DO THAT.

"This was not supposed to happen."

Rory Gilmore

S5 E2 A MESSENGER, NOTHING MORE

EVERYDAY LIFE

If you don't want it found, don't leave it around

When you've got a secret-filled letter, don't leave it around, and make sure it doesn't fall into the wrong hands. When Rory writes Dean an emotional letter about their affair, his wife, Lindsay, finds it in his jacket pocket. Lorelai writes a heartfelt letter about Luke to help him get joint custody of April and leaves one of her rough drafts in a drawer, where Christopher finds it and realizes she still loves Luke. If you're hiding a secret letter, have a think about why you're hiding it in the first place. There might be a conversation waiting to be had that shouldn't be a secret after all.

"Stars Hollow was a better place before Jess got here."

Taylor Doose
S2 E8 THE INS AND OUTS OF INNS

EVERYDAY LIFE

Everyone has more going on than you realize

Before you judge somebody, take a minute to look beneath the surface. Everyone treats Jess like a vandal, but behind that Holden Caulfield persona is a kid who feels abandoned by his parents. Jess doesn't trust anyone, which is likely why he gives Luke a hard time, doesn't pay attention in school, antagonizes Lorelai, and steals a gnome from Babette's garden. Rory gives Jess a chance right from the beginning, which helps them develop a true connection. Everybody's got a story, even if they don't tell you about it, so be kind.

"Do not mock my Pro/Con list!"

Rory Gilmore
S6 E17 I'M OK, YOU'RE OK

EVERYDAY LIFE

The pros and cons of the Pro/Con list

Pro: It's an opportunity to think things through step-by-step.

Con: It's a stalling tactic dressed up as a thoughtful process.

Pro: It slows things down. You can take a breath.

Con: It slows things down, and you need a decision.

Pro: You get to make a list!

Con: You have to make a list.

"Avril Lavigne rocks! You are such a snob."

Kyon

S6 E19 I GET A SIDEKICK OUT OF YOU

EVERYDAY LIFE

Don't be a gatekeeper

Are you an expert on movies? Music? Edgar Allan Poe? Being a fan is all well and good until you start making rules about who else gets to be one. That's called gatekeeping, whether it's about the Macarena, Maroon 5, or Mira Sorvino. Lane and Rory are offenders in this category. Rory's disappointed in Bono for touring with No Doubt, and Zack sneaks over to Sophie's music shop to play bluegrass because he's afraid of Lane's judgment. Love what you love, be who you want to be, and let everyone else do the same.

Lorelai's pop culture reference guide

LOVE & RELATIONSHIPS

★ *Lady and the Tramp* (this 1955 animated movie had a famous scene where the two dogs eat a strand of spaghetti from each end until they're kissing)

★ "One is the loneliest number" (from the song "One," a 1969 hit for Three Dog Night)

FAMILY & FRIENDSHIP

★ Thelma and Louise (an inseparable, ride-or-die movie duo)

★ Joel and Ethan (the movie-making Coen brothers)

★ Damon and Affleck (movie-making best buds Matt and Ben)

★ Wile E. Coyote (a character from the *Looney Tunes* cartoons)

★ Golden ticket (from *Willy Wonka & the Chocolate Factory*)

MONEY

★ Rosalind Russell (a film star who never made a movie with Ava Gardner)

★ Ava Gardner (a film star who never made a movie with Rosalind Russell)

SCHOOL & WORK

- ★ Captain Ahab (a main character in Herman Melville's *Moby Dick*)
- ★ "Danger, Will Robinson!" (a catchphrase from 1960s TV series *Lost in Space*)
- ★ Don Corleone (a character in *The Godfather* movies, played by Marlon Brando)

FOOD (& COFFEE)

- ★ Alain Ducasse (a French chef and restaurant owner)
- ★ Billy Joel (a singer/songwriter)
- ★ Viggo Mortenson (an American actor Luke mistakenly calls Vito Morgenstern)
- ★ *Willy Wonka & the Chocolate Factory* (a 1971 movie starring Gene Wilder)
- ★ *Mystic Pizza* (a 1988 movie starring Julia Roberts)
- ★ *Ratatouille* (a 2007 animated movie about a rat that can cook)

DREAMS & ASPIRATIONS

★ Bono (the lead singer of rock band U2)

EVERYDAY LIFE

★ *Fiddler on the Roof* (a hit Broadway musical that Lulu's students put on at school)

★ Holden Caulfield (the angsty main character in J. D. Salinger's novel *Catcher in the Rye*)

★ Macarena (a dance craze in the mid '90s)

★ Maroon 5 (a pop group)

★ Mira Sorvino (an actor who graduated from Harvard)

★ No Doubt (a rock band)

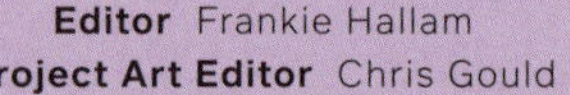

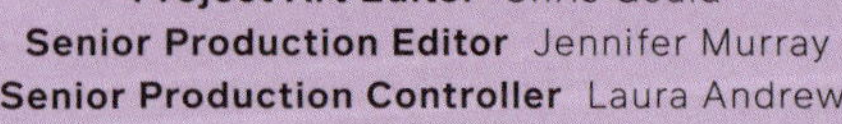

Editor Frankie Hallam
Project Art Editor Chris Gould
Senior Production Editor Jennifer Murray
Senior Production Controller Laura Andrews
Managing Editor Rachel Lawrence
Managing Art Editor Vicky Short
Managing Director Mark Searle

Designed for DK by Lisa Robb

DK would like to thank: Victoria Selover and Katie Campbell at Warner Bros. Discovery, Julia March and Jennette ElNaggar for proofreading, and Matt Jones for editorial assistance.

First published in Great Britain in 2024 by Dorling Kindersley Limited
DK, One Embassy Gardens, 8 Viaduct Gardens, London SW11 7BW

The authorised representative in the EEA is
Dorling Kindersley Verlag GmbH. Arnulfstr. 124,
80636 Munich, Germany

10 9 8 7 6 5 4 3 2 1
001–339696–Sep/2024

A CIP catalogue record for this book
is available from the British Library.
ISBN: 978-0-2416-6159-8

Printed and bound in China
www.dk.com

This book was made with Forest Stewardship Council™ certified paper – one small step in DK's commitment to a sustainable future.
Learn more at www.dk.com/uk/information/sustainability

“I’ve seen the way he looks at you, the way you look at him.”

Emily Gilmore

S1 E14 THAT DAMN DONNA REED